Role of Space-Time in Jaina's Syādvāda & Quantum Theory

Sri Garib Das Oriental Series No. 172

Role of Space-Time in Jaina's Syādvāda & Quantum Theory

Filita Bharucha

Sri Satguru Publications
A Division of
Indian Books Centre
Shakti Nagar, Delhi
India

The research work of this Book, `Role of Space-Time in Jainas Syādvāda and Quantum Theory' is undertaken under the auspicies of the Indian Council of Philosophical Research with the Director (P & R), Dr. Ranjan K. Ghosh by Dr. Filita Bharucha as a General Fellow Scholar with the assistance of the Research Supervisor, Dr. S.G. Mudgal, working in the Anantacharya Indological Research Institute having the well-known Director Dr. K.K.A. Venkatachari.

Published by:
Sri Satguru Publications
Indological and Oriental Publishers
A Division of
Indian Books Centre
40/5, Shakti Nagar,
Delhi-110007
(INDIA)

First Edition: Delhi, 1993

ISBN 81-7030-384-2

Laser Typeset by: ShiKi Associates, New Delhi.

Printed in India

Foreword

The main significance of this book is to emphasize the role of space and time and the importance of "indeterminacy" played by Syādvāda in Jainas Philosophy along with the Physicist Heiserberg's "Uncertaincy Principle" in Quantum Mechanics. Also with the importance of the unification of Space-Time by the great physicist and philosopher Einstein. For further information I have provided "truth-tables" of Jainas Syādvāda and Quantum Logic.

This book is written in view of the Einstein Theory regarding the unification of space-time and its role of the ancient schools (mainly Jainas) in perceptive of the modern age and also shows that the quantum theory which has to be of further advancement in view of the logical operations which created an empirical new standpoint of the world. In fact the book discusses how the Eastern and Western thoughts of space and time which is simultaneously play part in the contemporary world.

In Chapter I, the advent of the 20th Century, ventures into ancient thinking of old schools who could visualise modern ideas of space and time and quantum theory theory.

In Chapter II, we in this book select the ancient schools of Jainas because I find it most suitable in view of the unification of space-time in the 20th century. The Jainas idea of space and time were exposed by their "Syādvāda Theory" of seven possibilities.

In Chapter III, shows that the macroscopic ideas of classical logic were not sufficient to microscopic fields, in respect of Quantum (Deviant) Logic. This is in view of the

In Chapter IV, we have a general survey of space-time and other aspects of varied ideas. The following are listed below:-

1. Role of Universal.
2. Thoughts Experiments.
3. *Reductio ad Absurdum.*

In Chapter V, we have the General Theories of Space-Time with a topological manifold and co-ordination of space-time.

Lastly, the conclusively Chapter VI, contains the paper that I have read in a seminar in Berlin (1992 July). It mentions the Heterologic angle with an empirical standpoint of (a) Probability in the physical sciences and (b) possibility in social sciences. However, in the above Chapter VI, at the moment, I select the probability section. Also I mentioned a matrix formulation of space-time and a geometrical structure of it.

The Reader is requested to note that no diacritical marks are made for Sanskrit words.

I wish you all a good reading and a serious thought of "indeterminacy" in our todays "Micro-World" passed by the jet-set world at the end of the 20th century. May be the `indeterminacy' of the `Micro-World' as it appears in today world, may change by the beginning of the 21st century. The `strict causality' of Newton, may loosen the causality in the 21st century.

Contents

Chapter-I

Advent of Space-Time

Before we begin discussing the Eastern and Western thoughts of space-time; we preliminary question the meaning of "thought", which is considered as "Logic as a science of thinking, which furnishes the mind with truth or knowledge."

Thinking being a conscious process that is built up and is a mode of action system which develop according to general laws of Organic evolution. Judgement, conception and inference on stages on evolution which is a transition to logic.

So far classical logic given yeomen service to the macroscopic field, but one cannot neglect the mysterious empirical nature of microscopic action in the later part of the 20th century. This brings up the transition of the Homologic (classical) to the Heterologic (modern) of our times. This is discussed in our Last Chapter of the book for the unification of space-time. The aim of my book is to show the empirical nature of Heterologic which is required for the later part of this century which is not only in the unification of space-time but the empirical element in quantum mechanics.

Many philosophical systems have attempted to describe the concepts of space and time. Plato included them in his world of ideas (the "higher" reality) Spinoza considered space as an attribute of God. Kant considered them as mere constructs of the human mind by means of which the observer combines his perception into an orderly fashion.

What can be said of the space-time continuum of Einstein? The answer we can give to the question on the basis of Einstein's theory of Relativity is very different from the answers of these philosophers. The theory of relativity shows that space and time a neither ideal objects nor forms of order of necessary for the human mind. They constitute a relational system expressing certain general features of physical objects and thus are descriptions of the physical world.

The space-time continuum of Einstein-Minkowski contains events which are interconnected by co-ordinates, but the connections between them are not necessarily causal. Any two events are represented by points in the space-time continuum. So far, I think that no connections between them are necessarily causal. Then how has the special relativity theory of Einstein modified our views on causality? Any two events are represented by points in the space-time continuum. So far, I think that no total ordering can be mathematically* defined on the infinite vector space (R^3 x T) (space-time continuum). However it is interesting to note that time alone forms continuum with an order type which is the order type of real numbers.

As we mentioned two events in (R^3 x T) are not comparable in this mathematical sense. However a partial ordering on T may enable us to have an ordering of time-like events in (R^3 x T) viz. event E_1 may be said to be earlier than event E_2 it $t_1 < t_2$. But then can E_1 be said to be a cause of E_2? Clearly mere contiguity in time does not establish a causal nexus; we should have causal operators (or relations) that justify the causal action (if any of E_1 and E_2.) The question then arises as what should be the nature of this causal operator? This is discussed in the last chapter.

Classical physics was dominated by the 2 independent concepts of space and time. They did not appear to have a

* Refer to the last chapter VI

functional dependence at all. However Einstein revolutionized the physical world by his introduction of the space-time embrace (as I call it). In the words of Minkowski in his lecture "Space and Time" in September 1908, "From now on the independent concept of time and the independent concept of space shall vanish as shadows and only a kind of union of them will preserve independence".

What can be said of the space-time continuum of Einstein? The answer we can give to the question on the basis of Einstein's theory of Relativity is very different from the answer of these philosophers. The theory of relativity shows that space and time are neither ideal object nor forms of order of necessary for the human mind. They constitute a relational system expressing certain general features of physical objects and thus are descriptions of the physical world. Therefore we note that the space-time continuum of Einstein-Minkowski contains events which are interconnected by co-ordinates.

The relativity theory heralded thee birth of the "spatio-temporal" manifold (lattice). The classical view before Einstein considered the time of an event in a system S' in arbitrary motion in relation to a system S as identical with the time of the same event as judged from the system S considered at rest. Clearly this can be expressed by the transformation equation t = t' which is required for classical laws of physics. For Newton, time had an absolute and mathematical flow regardless of relation to any object. Einstein stepped out to show to that his hypothesis was not tenable.

As a consequence of the space-time interlink, Einstein could show that local measurements are not universal. They could be used to obtain universal laws by composing them with local measurements of other systems. By examining certain relationships, between local measurements which remain unchanged with reference to all systems moving with velocity with respect to each other. Therefore, one arrives at the invariants of our universe.

By emphasising that absolute space and absolute time are myths and that the only practical notions of time that man can have, are obtained by some method of signals, Einstein shows that "idealism" or "a priori thinking" is not sufficient for investigating the universe. On the other hand, since actual measurements are local and not universal, the Einstein theory shows that the measurement (experiment) in a given frame alone is not sufficient.

In conclusion we see that special relativity pointed out that things which appear alike to two observers moving relative to each other than uniform velocity, are the facts of the universe.

Chapter II

Jaina's View of Reality as Modern Thoughts of Space and Time

Before we begin the actual theory of *Syādvāda* of Jainism in relevance to its connection in relations with space and time and how its resembles the space-time unification in the 20th century, we shall start with its epistemological background.

The Jainas bring the whole universe under one or other of two everlasting categories. The two class of things are respectively described as *jiva* and *ajiva*, i.e. the conscious and the unconscious or spirit and non-spirit the latter including not merely matter but also time and space. The terms show clearly the realistic and relativistic standpoint of Jainism. As surely as is a subject that know, Jainism says, so surely is there an object that is known. Of them, the ajiva has its own specific nature, but that nature cannot be properly understood until it is contrasted with the *jiva*. That is why it is designated as 'not-jiva' or the contradictory of *jiva*. The latter is the higher and more important category, which accounts for its independent designation, although that also can be well understood only when contrasted with the *ajiva* or non-spirit:

(1) *Jiva* - The notion of jiva in general corresponds to that of at man or purpose of the other schools of Indian thought. But as implied by the etymology of its name 'what lives is animate' - the concept seems to have been arrived at first by observing the characteristics of life and not through the search after a metaphysical principle underlying individual existence. The Jainas believe not only that the *jiva* exists but also that it

acts and is acted upon. It is both an experient (*bhokta*) and an agent (*karta*). Its intrinsic nature is one of perfection and it is characterized by infinite intelligence, infinite peace, infinite faith and infinite power. One of the curious features of Jainism is the belief in the variable size of the jiva in its empirical condition. It is capable of expansion and contraction according to the dimensions of the physical body with which it is associated for the *time* being.

Finishing the discussion of the Jiva we shall concentrate on the ajiva because of its relevance to space and time.

(2) *Ajiva*–The category of *ajiva* is divided into *kala* (time), *akasa*, *dharma* and *adharma* (which together may for our purpose be regarded as standing for 'space') and *pudgala* (matter). The essential distinction from the *jiva* is that they, as such lack life and consciousness. Of these *time* is infinite. But there are cycles in it, each cycle having two eras of equal duration described as the avasarpini and the utsarpini a metaphor drawn from the revolving wheel. The former is the descending era in which the reverse take place. The present era is stated to be the former. Space which also is *infinite* is conceived of as being in two parts-one (*alokakasa*) where movement is possible and the other (*alokakasa*) where it is not. Whatever is, only in the former and the latter is empty *akasa*, an abyss of nothing, stretching infinitely beyond it. The changes or modes are known as *paryayas*, which as distinguished from the enduring substance, come into being, persist for at least one instant and then disappear. The term dravya or 'substance' is applied to the six entities mentioned above - the *jiva* and the *ajiva* with its five-fold division. The dravyas, excepting *time* alone, are called *asti-kayas*, a term which means that they are real in the sense just explained (*asti*) and possess by infinite intelligence, infinite peace, infinite faith and infinite power.

Jainas speak about reality of experience and experience as a character of reality.

In connection of this view of reality we formulate the *theory of Syādvāda* in terms of *modern ideas of logic.*

Therefore we seek to investigate whether a 3-valued deviant (extended) logic which can represent the *Syādvāda* theory of Jainism. If so, can the epistemological implications regarding the description of an object in the phenomenal world in terms of a *pramana* (complete judgement) which, according to the Jains, is an always true statement, be interpreted in terms of a 3 valued deviant logic leading to a tautology?

Syādvāda, the doctrine of the relativism of judgments states that all actual and possible assertions in regard to an object are relative and therefore conditionally true or false. An individual's judgement about a thing or event need not only be valid for anyone other than the subject himself, but is also conditioned by its *relationship* to a point of *space* and *time*, and by its *mode* and *substance.*

Pramāna or complete judgement describes the object in the phenomenal world with all its seven possibilities which are stated by the Jainas as follows:

(i) May be, it is (*Syādasti*);
(ii) may be, it is not (*Syād-nāsti*);
(iii) may be, it is and it is not different times (*Syād-asti-nāsti*);
(iv) may be, it is and it is not at the same time which means that its indescribable (*Syād-avaktavya*);
(v) may be, it is and yet indescribable (*Syād-asti-avaktavya*);
(vi) may be, it is not and also indescribable (*Syād-asti-avaktavya*);

(vii) may be, it is and it is not and also indescribable (*Syād-asti-nāsti avaktavya*),

The above seven possibilities comprise the theory of *Syādavāda* (*Saptabhangi naya*) and describe an object X of the phenomenal world subject to the factors of space, time, mode and substance from seven standpoints. However, the above seven predications must be consistent with the facts of objective reality and be bases on the principles of affirmation and negation. We note that an object is conditioned by the factors of space, time, mode and substance, hence the affirmation and the negation of a proposition regarding it are to be assigned suitable truth-values. Also, since the third, sixth and seventh, predications involve the concept of simultaneity and non-simultaneity (with accounts for the object being conditioned by time), we have changed the meanings of the connectives 'and' 'and' 'or'. As a matter of fact, we have introduced two varieties of 'and', one symbolised by 'A' (simultaneous conjunction), the other 'and' is symbolised by (non-simultaneous conjunction). As for the connective 'or' symbolised by Λ we shall use the meaning assigned to it by Reichenbach in his 3-valued logic introduced by him to describe various anomalies in quantum mechanics.

2. Logical Analysis of *Saptabhangi-naya*:

Mallisena distinguished a *pramana* from a *durnaya* and a *naya*. According to him, a *pramana* is always true and for which we assign the truth-value T, but durnaya is always false for which we assign truth-value F. The truth value of a naya (incomplete judgement) is different from the truth-value T or the truth-value F hence it is intermediate between these two truth-values. This gives rise to a third intermediate truth value I.

According to Vadi Devasuri's *Pramāna-Tattvalokālam kāra*, (3 *loc cit*) the above seven predications can be interpreted as follows:

The first predication consist of an affirmative statement. This may mean that an object exists in some respects. The expression 'in some respects' is to be taken in the context of various factors like space, time, substance and mode. For instance, the substance of an object X could be related to the material of which it is made. The space relates to the spatial location of X. The time of existence of X is the present time at which it exists. The mode of X descrites its configuration.

Let us represent, the first affirmative predication by a proposition P which takes a truth value T.

The second predication consists of a negative statement that 'in some respects' an object X is non-existent. Here the word 'may be' (*syād*) or 'in some respects' is crucial in respect of assigning the truth-value to this predication. The elucidate that the object X may not exist with reference to either space, time, substance or mode we note that on account of restrain called diametrical connective(*) *i.e.* in some respects'. We shall consider the connective of negation ($\urcorner$) as a 'complete' negation and not as a 'dimetrical' negation in the sense of Reichenbach. Let us represent the second predication by the proposition $\urcorner$P which takes the truth value, I, as shown by the following truth-table

(Reichenbach 4 *loc cit*)

Truth Table No. I

P	$\urcorner$P
T	I
I	I
F	T

The third predication consists of affirmative and negative statements conjunctively made one after another. Since the affirmative proposition P and complete negative proposition $\neg P$ are taken conjunctively one after another we assign the truth-value T to the non-simultaneous conjunction of the affirmative proposition P and the negative proposition $\neg P$. We denote this non-simultaneous conjunction of P and $\neg P$ by the notation $(P \bullet \neg P)$.

The fourth predication consists of affirmative and negative statements made simultaneously. Since an object X is incapable of being expressed in terms of existence and non-existence at the same time even allowing for *Syād*, it is termed 'indescribable'. Hence we assign to the fourth predication which is the simultaneous conjunction of the affirmative proposition P and the negative proposition $\neg P$, the indeterminate truth-value I and denote the statement corresponding to the fourth predication as $(P \wedge \neg P.)$

The fifth predication consists in an affirmative statement conjoined with an indescribable statement at the same time. We denote this fifth predication by $P \wedge (P \wedge \neg P)$.

Referring to the column for simultaneous conjunction in the truth-table that follows:

We see that since P takes the truth-value T by the first predication and $(P \wedge \neg P)$ is assigned the truth-value I by the fourth predication, the proposition $P \wedge (P \wedge \neg P)$ takes the truth Value I

The sixth predication consists of a negative statement conjoined with an indescribable statement at the same time. We denote this sixth predication by $(\neg P) \wedge (P \wedge \neg P)$. Referring to the column for the simultaneous conjunction $(\wedge)$ in the table given above, we see that since $\neg P$ takes the truth-value I by the second predication and $(P \wedge \neg P)$ is assigned the truth-value I by the fourth predication we see that the proposition $\neg P\ (P \wedge \neg P)$ takes the truth-value I.

Truth Table No. 2

A	B	A • B	A Λ B	A V B
T	T	T	T	T
T	I	T	I	T
T	F	T	I	T
I	T	T	I	T
I	I	T	I	I
I	F	F	F	I
F	T	T	I	T
F	I	F	F	I
F	F	F	F	F

The seventh or the last predication consists of an affirmative and negative statements made non-simultaneously conjoined simultaneously with the affirmative and the negative statement conjoined simultaneously. This statement is denoted by $(P \bullet \rceil P) \wedge (P \wedge \rceil P)$. Referring to the columns for the connectives for simultaneous conjunction and for non-simultaneous conjunction in the truth-table No. 2 and nothing that P takes the truth-value T by the first predication and $\rceil P$ takes the truth value I by the second predication. We see that $(P \bullet \rceil P)$ takes the true-value T (third predication) and $(P \wedge \rceil P)$ takes the truth-value I (fourth predication). The seventh predication thus takes the truth-value I according to the same truth-tables.

Hence, we see that the *pramana saptabhangi* of the Jainas is a table of seven statements which are derived from a true statement by the operations of negation, non-simultaneous and simultaneous conjunctions that are denoted by $\rceil$, •, Λ, respectively.

Let us consider P as a true statement then the pramana-saptabhangi can be represented as follows:

(1) P (assertion of P)
(2) Not P ('complete' negation of P) denoted by $\neg P$
(3) P and non-simultaneously not P (non-simultaneous conjunction of P and ($\neg P$) denoted by $P \bullet \neg P$
(4) P and simultaneously not P (simultaneous conjunction of P and $\neg P$) denoted by $(P \wedge \neg P)$.
(5) P and simultaneously (P and simultaneously not P) denoted $P \wedge (P \wedge \neg P)$.
(6) Not P and simultaneously not (P and simultaneously not P) denoted by $\neg P \wedge (P \wedge \neg P)$.
(7) (P and non-simultaneously not P) and simultaneously (P and simultaneously not P) denoted by $(P \bullet \neg P) \wedge (P \wedge \neg P)$.

Pictorially we can depict the pramana-saptabhangi as follows ($\neg$ seven view points)

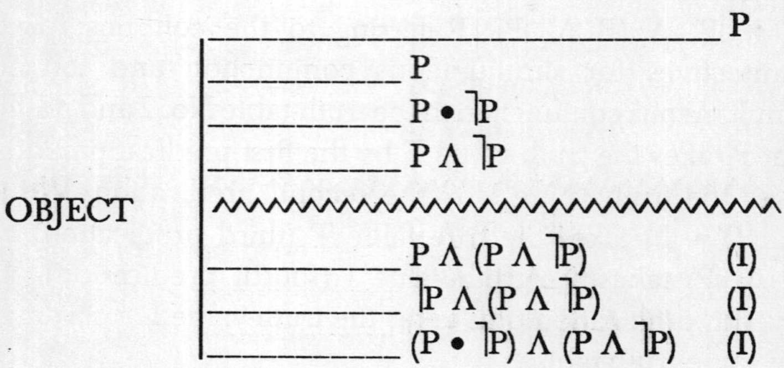

An object X can be view from any one of these seven standpoints. However, since the totally of all these seven possibilities comprises the *pramana-Saptabhangi* (complete judgement of the phenomenal world in terms of seven possibilities), the conjunction, denoted, by V, of these seven predications should lead to a tautology. We can present this disjunction as follows:

$$(P \vee \neg P) \vee (P \bullet \neg P) \vee (P \wedge \neg P) \vee [P \wedge (P \wedge \neg P)] \vee [(\neg P) \wedge (P \wedge \neg P)] \vee [(P \bullet \neg P) \wedge (P \wedge \neg P)]$$

As we have noted earlier, the seven predications, conjoined by the disjunction above, take the truth-values T, I, T, I, I, I respectively. Referring to the column for the disjunction in the truth-value No.2 and nothing that the disjunction is associative as can be easily checked using the same truth-table, we see that the disjunction of all these seven predications is indeed a tautology taking the truth-value T.

Accordingly the seven-fold argument of *Syādvāda* theory of Jainism which is supposed to exhaust all the possibilities of describing the objective reality and lead to a complete description (*Pramāna*) of the phenomenal world in terms of an always true statement can be represented as a tautology with respect to our deviant logic.

The Jains were not aware of the fact that the relativism they were proponding suggests a verdict of disfavour of all knowledge obtained and obtained and obtainable by us in the phenomenal world. For a world which is devisible into an ever exhaustible number of points of view and whose entitely we never comprehend is just inaccessible to empirical sensibilities or rational statements. Does this suggest that we require an infinite-valued deviant logic to represent the Jains epistemology or perhaps it is beyond the scope of logic.

Chapter III

Role of Quantum Theory in Deviant Logic

This Chapter shows that the macroscopic ideas of a classical logic were not sufficient to microscopic fields to needed for Quantum Theory for space-time unification. Before this, we discuss shortly that how ancient ideas of Jainas come about.

The atomic theory of Jainas play a part in someway for quantum logic. The word '*anu*' the Sanskrit equivalent* of 'atom', where these atoms are all believed to house souls and the entire universe is full of them.

The atoms, according to it, are all of the same kind, but they can yet give rise to the infinite variety of things so that matter as conceived here is of quite an indefinite nature. Pudgala has, as we know, certain inalienable features; but within the limits imposed by them it can become anything though qualitative differentiation. The transmutation of the elements is quite possible in this view and is not a mere dream of the alchemist. These so-called elements also, according to Jainism, are divisible and have a structure. By developing the respective characteristics of odour, flavour, etc., the atoms become differentiated, though in themselves they are indistinguishable from one another, and it is form the atoms diversified in this way that the rest of the material world is derived. Matter may thus have to formsôone, simple or atomic and the other compound called skandha. All perceivable objects are of the latter kind.

* The term `equivalent' must be taken with a finish of slat. It is mainly with a translatory meaning.

We have completed the Jainas ancient view of atoms, then we shall introduce the microscopic fields of the quantum world.

The problem of transition from quantum to classical behaviour of physical system lies at the heart of all concentrate problems and paradoxes associated with the interpretation of quantum theory.

In the latter 20th century, the indeterministic world was accepted by most scientist. The causality of nature was not taken seriously. According to the dominant paradigm man have reached to the capacity of understanding macroscopic to phenomena.

In this chapter we discuss the problem of measurement in quantum theory by the way of deviant logic mainly by discussing the *operational meaning* of logical connectives. Since we are dealing with the quantum world, our deviant logic will be quantum logic.

In this chapter we have attempted to present the logic of quantum mechanics by examining the measurement process in quantum mechanics to determine the meanings of the logical connectives and to find whether they retain the meanings in the light of strange new features of the quantum mechanical measurement processes. Most authors of quantum logic, particularly Finkelsten and Putnam have emphasized the fact that connectives in quantum logic retain classical meanings on account of operational definitions, though quantum logic differs from classical logic in only one respect. It is the failure of the distributive law: $\alpha \Lambda (\beta V \gamma) = (\alpha V \beta) V (\alpha \Lambda \gamma)$ of the classical logic. We find in our investigations that in view of the peculiar nature of quantum mechanical measurements, the meanings of the logical connectives needed to conjoin simple experimental propositions to form compound statements need changes. It is seen that with the new meanings given to the logical connectives, this distributive law remains valid.

Experimental Propositions of Quantum Mechanics: It is well known that in classical mechanics the state of a mechanical system at any time is completely known if one specifies in generalized coordinates 'q' and in generalized momenta 'p' at that time, where is the number of degrees of freedom of the mechanical system. There can be obtained by solving Hamilton's equations of motion with the initial conditions specified by the values of 'q' and 'p' at time t = o. Quantum mechanical state of microscopic systems is represented by a certain wave-function ψ (or a state vector 1x>) which can be explained as a linear combination of eigenfunctions ui (or eigenvectors | i> |) of an operator representing an observable. The wave-function ψ (or the state vector x>) is obtained by solving a differential equation known as Schrodinger equation which is of first order in time, the initial condition being the value of ψ at time t = 0. In what follows we accept quantum mechanics in its conventional form as the correct representation of the microworld and accordingly build up our formalism.

Let an observable in quantum mechanics be denoted by A with the corresponding Hermitian operator denoted by the same letter A for convenience. We know from quantum mechanics that A must possess sufficient number of eigenstates, often infinite, that any state vector whatever can be expanded in terms of the corresponding eigen-vectors. The spectrum of the corresponding eigenvalues may be discreet (finite or denumerably infinite, degenerat or non-degenerate) of continuous. For our analysis we shall assume that the eigenvalue spectra of all the operators we shall introduce, be discrete, finite and non-degenerate. Let the eigenvectors of A be noted by | a> where i = 1, 2...., n (< ∞). If A represented an observable, then any arbitrary state vector 1x> can be expanded as

$$|x\rangle = \sum_{i=1}^{n} |a_i\rangle\langle a_i|x\rangle$$

If a_i denote the eigenvalues of A for the states $|a_i\rangle$, then $A|a_i\rangle = a_i|a_i\rangle$. The process of measurement in quantum mechanics consists of three successive stages; (1) A preparatory stage when the quantum mechanical system S is 'prepared' to be in an arbitrary state $|x\rangle$, considered as the initial state; (2) a working stage in which the 'prepared' system S interacts with the measuring apparatus (a macroscopic body), we shall call the analyzer and goes over to the superposition state

$$|x\rangle = \sum_{i=1}^{n} |a_i\rangle\langle a_i|x\rangle$$

and (3) a registering stage in which the system S is registered in one of the eigenstates forming the superposition in the above expression (reduction of the wavepacket). Hence the process of measurement can be described as

$$(1)\ |x\rangle = (2) \sum_{i=1}^{n} |a_i\rangle\langle a_i|x\rangle\ (3)\,|a_i\rangle$$

Experimental Proposition (EP) is a statement of the form: "The result of a measurement on a system S in the state $|x\rangle$ and for the observable A is" The completion of the sentence can be made in two ways, (1) "a real number ai giving the value of the real dynamical A at time" and (2) "... that the system, after the measurement is complete, is described by the state vector $|a_i\rangle$", If the statement is completed in the manner (1), we shall call that statement as the experimental proposition of the first kind (EP I) and denote by, say, α_i if the statement is completed in the manner (2), we shall call that statement as the experimental proposition of the second kind (EP II) and denote it by α_i'. Thus (EP 1) is of the form M (SA1x> = ai) and (EP II) is of the form M (S A (x.) = 1ai>. In the present paper, we shall concern ourselves with EP 1's only and drop the suffixes I and II.

Experimental Meaning of Logical Connectives:

In this section we shall consider the problem of introducing this compound statements involving two or more EP's of the type described in the previous section and giving experimental meaning to the logical connectives conjoining them. We first consider the case of an observable represented by the Hermitian operator A with the eigen-value spectrum, a_1 a_2.... a_n, 1a_1 1a_2>.... 1_n> are the eigenvectors of A belonging to these eigenvalues. We assume to make measurement on identical copies of the system S prepared to be in the same state 1x> to measure the observable A. We denote, as in section 2, the EP's M (S A1x>) = a_i as α_i. The aforementioned measurements will furnish the results a_1 or a_2 or a_3 or ...., not necessarily in that order, with probability measure associated with each of them. This means that a_1 or a_2 or ..... , are the possible (exclusive) results of the measurement process. If we put n = 2, then we may say that result of this measurement is either a_1 or a_2 but never both at the same time, when measurements are repeated on the identical samples in the same state. This measurement statement (for n = 2) can be translated into the logical language as α_1 V α_2 where the connective 'V' is used in the exclusive sense. Let B be another observable with the corresponding Hermitian operator B with the complete set of eigenvectors 1b_i>. This observable may or may not be compatible with the observable A. The measurements on identical copies of S in the state 1 x_i> to measure A and B not simultaneously, but successively, should give the results as a_is or b_is occurring singly at a time. Such measurement results can be put into the logical language as α_i V β_i with 'V' again in the exclusive sense where the EP β_i is M (Sβ1x>) = b_i. The results of successive measurements of one or more observables on identical copies of a quantum mechanical system, all prepared to be in a given state, are expressible in terms of an exclusive disjunction given by the truth-table 1.

Truth-Table I

Having given the experimental meaning to disjunction, we now turn to the connective 'L' symbolizing conjunction. Let L and M be Hermitian operators corresponding to two observables.

Let the discrete eigenvectors of these operators be denoted by li> and |m1 and the corresponding eigenvalues to which they belong be 1_1 and m_1. The indices i and j run through discrete integral values. Obviously |li> and | mi> form a complete set of eigenvectors. We want to give meaning to the problem of simultaneous measurement of two observables. Suppose an experiment to measure simultaneously the values of L and M is performed on a system S in an arbitrary state 1 x>, we shall consider the result as read on two guages - L-guage and M-guage-simultaneously. We imagine this as some kind of coincidence measurement technique used with L-guage and M-guage expected to respond at the same time. If we denote the EP M (S L| x>) = l_i as λ_i, and M (SM1 | x>) = m_j as μ_j then the L-guage reading li and M-guage reading mi gives the experimental proposition the results of the simultaneous measurement of L and M on S in the state 1 x> are the real numbers l_i and m_j. This EP can be translated into the logical language as λi Λ μj. Hence the measurement of two observables furnishes us with the EP which is conjunction of two EP's.

In studying conjunction we must distinguish between cases: (1) when the two operators commute i.e. the corresponding observables are compatible and (2) when the two operators do not commute and the corresponding observables are incompatible.

Case (1) Let the two commuting operators be denoted by A and B, they satisfy (A, B) = 0. We know from a well-known theorem in quantum mechanics that A and B have a common complete set of eigenvectors, hence we put $|a_1\rangle = |b_1\rangle = |a_i\ bj\rangle|$, where we have indicated the common set of eigenvectors as $|a_1\ b_1\rangle$ in which the letters a_1 and b_1 with the same subscript 'i' are inserted with the ket symbol $1\rangle$ signifying that the ket $|a_i\ b_1\rangle$ is an eigenket of both A and B. Since A and B are observables, we have

$$1x\rangle = \sum_{i=1}^{n} |a_i b_i\rangle\langle a_i b_i\rangle\ |x\rangle$$

A simultaneous measurement of A and B on the system S in the state $1\ x\rangle$ will furnish some ai as the reading of A-guage and some b_i of the B-guage simultaneously, where $A\ |a_1\ b_1\rangle = a_i\ |\ a_i\ b_i\rangle$ and $B\ 1\ a_i\ b_i\rangle = b_i\ |a_i\ b_i\rangle$ (reduction of the wave packet). In the logical language, this is $\alpha_i \wedge \beta_i$. We note that the index-set 1, such that $i \in I$, is so arranged that the results of the above measurements are $a_1 b_1$. This means that when A-guage reads a_i, B-guage reads b_i. It never happens that the results are a_i and b_i with $i \neq j$, hence the statement $a_i \wedge b_j$ $(i \neq j)$ is always false in this case. To construct the truth-table for conjunction '$\wedge$' in the case of compatible observables, we consider the experimental set-up with two coincidence guages to read the values of A and B. If the A-guage reads a_i and B-guage simultaneously reads b_i, then we assign the truth value T to both α_i and β_i and $\alpha_i \wedge \beta_i$ is also assigned the truth value T. If the A-guage registered reading a_1, but B-guage does not register anything, we shall assign the truth value T to α_i, F to β_j and F to $\alpha_i \Lambda \beta_j$. The reason is that by the very nature of the coincidence technique, this may be considered as the apparatus malfunction and the corresponding reading is rejected. So also if we assign F to α_i, T to β_j then $\alpha_i \Lambda \beta_j$ has the truth value F. Lastly, if both guages fail to respond, we assign F to α_i F to β_j and F to $\alpha_i \Lambda \beta_j$ leading to the truth table 2.

Truth-Table 2

We see that the above truth table coincides with that classical logic.

Case (2): Let the two non-commuting Hermitian operators be noted by P and Q. These correspond to two incompatible observables. Let P and Q satisfy [P, Q] = iR, where R is also a Hermitian operator corresponding to an observable. We denote the EP "the result of the measurement of P on S in the state 1 x> is P_1 (a real eigenvalue) as ϕ_i and the EP "the result of the measurement of Q on S in the state 1x > is q_1 (a real eigenvalue) as ψ_i". In these EP's the results of measurements of P and Q are supposed to have the sharp values p_1 and q_1 with standard deviations Δp and Δq equal to zero. According to the uncertainty principle, if P and ϕ are measured simultaneously, $\Delta p \, \Delta q \geq ½$ where r is the expectation value of R in state 1 x>. From this we see that ϕ_i is true if $\Delta p = 0$ and ψ_j is true if $\Delta = 0$, but φ_i is false if $\Delta p \neq 0$ and ψ_j is false if $\Delta q \neq 0$*. From the uncertainty principle, it is clear that $\phi \Lambda \phi_j$ is false only in the case when both ϕ_i and ψ_j are true, but it is true otherwise, resulting in the truth-table 3.

Truth Table 3

* In fact for clarity, one may say that ϕ_i is true if $\Delta p < \frac{r}{2\Delta q}$ and ψ_j is true if $\Delta q < \frac{r}{2\Delta p}$; but ϕ_i is false if $\Delta p \geq \frac{r}{2\Delta q}$ and ψ_j is false if $\Delta q \geq \frac{r}{2\Delta p}$.

For the purpose of extending the analysis to more than two EP's conjoined by the disjunction 'V', let us consider a Hermitian operator A corresponding to some observable. An EP of the form M (SA1x) = a_1 is denoted by i, i = 1, 2, 3 .... n(< ∞). We know from quantum mechanics that the system can be only in one state at a time. Hence at some time if α_i ($| \leq i \leq n$) is true than all the other α_k's with $K \neq i$ are false at that time. We write α_1 V α_2 V α_3.... α_n to mean that the system S has the property described by the observable A. Similarly from another Hermitian operator B with the spectrum of eigenvalues β_1 β_2...., β_m (in general m an EP of the form M ($S_{B\lambda x>}$) = b_i> will be denoted by β_i. Using the same argument, we consider β_1 V β_2 V β_3.... β_n as an always true statement to mean that the system S has the property described by the observable B. Clearly in the above expressions, we see that the disjunction is true if only one disjunct is false if two ore more of the disjuncts are true at a time. This is the requirement of an exclusive disjunction we have introduced in our quantum logic.

Regarding the connective 'Λ' signifying conjunction, we cannot extend its meanings to a statement of the form α Λ β γ Λ.... of more than two EP's as this statement cannot be given a meaning, particularly for incompatible observables, since it refers to the result of simultaneous measurement of more than two observables. Even thee quantum mechanics such measurements are hardly required and discussed. As the connective iΛ' conjoins two EP's which express the result of simultaneous measurement of two observable on a system S in an arbitrary state, we consider a statement of the form α_i Λ α_j as always false, where α_i and α_j are the EP's corresponding to the same observables. This is due to the fact that if α_i is true, α_j is false and that an observable is compatible with itself which follows the truth-table 2. However, the statement "the system has the properties described by the observables A and B at the same time will be described by the expression $(\alpha_1 \vee \alpha_2 \vee \alpha_3 .... \alpha_n) \wedge (\beta_1 \vee \beta_2 \vee \beta_3 \vee .... \vee \beta_m)$ according to the meaning given to the connective '$\wedge$'. If A and B are compatible observables, the expression $(\alpha_1 \vee \alpha_2 \vee .... \vee \alpha_n) \wedge (\beta_1 \vee \beta_2 \vee .... \beta_n)$ where we have put m = n, is an always true statement. If P and Q are incompatible observables with the corresponding EP's denoted by ϕ and ψ then the statements $(\phi_1 \vee \phi_2 \vee \phi_3 .... \phi_n)$ and $(\psi_1 \vee \psi_2 \vee .... \psi_m$ are always true, but the statement $(\phi_1 \vee \phi_2 \vee .... \vee \phi_n) \wedge (\psi_1 \vee \psi_2 \vee .... \psi_m)$ where, in general $m \neq n$, signifying that the system has the properties P an Q at the same time, is an always false statement. It is often implied that a quantum mechanical system S simultaneously possess properties described by the compatible observables P and Q at all times and that it is the measurement process that introduces the uncertainty. This is evidently false as the above results shows.

4. The Distributive Law: In the classical logic, we have two different forms of the distributive law. We shall state each forms for the two cases below. The generalization is obvious.

One form is

(I) $\alpha \vee (\beta \wedge \gamma) = (\alpha \vee \beta) \wedge (\alpha \vee \gamma)$ and

(I) $(\alpha \wedge \beta) \vee (\gamma \wedge \delta) =$

$$(\alpha \vee \gamma) \wedge (\alpha \vee \delta) \wedge (\alpha \vee \delta) \wedge (\beta \vee \gamma) \wedge (\beta \vee \delta)$$

The other form is

(II) $\alpha \wedge (\beta \vee \gamma) = (\alpha \wedge \beta) \vee (\alpha \wedge \gamma)$

(II) $(\alpha \vee \beta) \wedge (\gamma \vee \delta) =$

$$(\alpha \wedge \gamma) \vee (\alpha \wedge \delta) \vee (\beta \wedge \rho) \vee (\beta \vee \delta)$$

First, let us consider the form (I). We apply it to two observables A and B with a complete spectrum of only one eigenvalue and two eigenvalues respectively. Then (I) can be written as $\alpha \vee (\beta_1 \wedge \beta_2) = (\alpha \vee \beta_i) \wedge (\alpha \vee \beta_2)$. In this expression we note, on the right hand side, there occur expression of the form (α V β_i) and (α V β_2) conjoined by the connective Λ. These expressions are obtained by conjoining two EP's corresponding to observables which may themselves in incompatible with other, so that it is impossible to say whether the EP's that correspond to (α V β_i) and (α V β_2) are compatible or incompatible with each other. There, within the scope of definition of the connective 'Λ' which has different truth-tables for compatible and incompatible observables, these EP's cannot be conjoined together by 'Λ'. This means that this form of the distributive law lies outside the ambit of our logical system. In any case, this form has not even been mentioned by Finkelstein and Putnam. Similarly in the expression $(\alpha_1 \Lambda \alpha_2) V (\beta_1 \Lambda \beta_2) = (\alpha_1 V \beta_1) \Lambda (\alpha_1 V \beta_2) \Lambda (\alpha_1 V \beta_2) \Lambda (\alpha_2 V \beta_1) \Lambda (\alpha_2 V \beta_2)$ the right hand side contains expressions (α_1 V β_1), (α_2 V β_2) conjoined by the connective 'Λ'. This expression involves more than two EP's conjoined by the connective 'Λ' to which it is not possible to give an empirical meaning. Besides the EP's (α_1 V β_1), (α_1 V β_2), may correspond to neither compatible nor incompatible observables and thus cannot be meaningfully conjoined together by the connective 'Λ'. Hence we shall speak no more about this form of the distributive law in this paper.

Secondly, we consider the form (II) which is the form admissible in our formalism of quantum logic. Here we shall distinguish between two cases: Case (1): The two observables A and B are compatible and the corresponding operators commute. Case (2): The two observables P and Q are incompatible and the corresponding operators do not commute.

We first consider case (1) In this case, we shall show that the distributive law holds when (a) the operator A has the complete spectrum of one eigenvalue and operator B has two (b) A has the spectrum of 2 eigenvalues, and B also has two and (c) A has the spectrum of 3 eigenvalues and B also has three. We shall show this by means of appropriate truth tables. (a) Let the EP M ($S_{A1x>}$) = a_i) be denoted by α and the EP: M ($S_{B1x>}$) = b by β_i, i = 1,2 .....n. In the case (a) we construct the following truth table 4.

Truth-Table 4

The truth values in the second and the seventh columns of the truth-table 4 show that the distributive law

$\alpha \wedge (\beta_1 \vee \beta_2) = (\alpha \wedge \beta_1) \vee (\alpha \wedge \beta_2)$ holds.

We now consider the case (b), where the operator A has the spectrum of two eigenvalues and B has also two. In this case we denote the EP's corresponding to the observable A as α_1 and α_2 and the EP's corresponding to the observable B as β_1 and β_2 the EP's Corresponding to the observables. For this case, we have the following truth-table 5.

Truth-Table 5

The truth values in the columns 4 and 12 in the truth-table 5 show that the distributive law holds. Finally, in the case (c) we denote the EP's corresponding to the observable A as α_1, α_2 and α_3 and the EP's corresponding to the observable B and β_1, β_2 and β_3. In this case we have the following truth-table 6.

Truth-Table 6

The truth values in the columns 8 and 19 in the truth-table 6 show that the distributive law holds even in this case. It is possible to construct truth-tables for more complex cases involving more than three eigenvalues each and see that the distributive law holds in all these cases.

Secondly, we consider the other case of incompatible observable. Again, here we look into (a) P has only one eigen-value and Q has two, (b) P has 2 eigenvalues. Q has also two and (c) P and 2 eigenvalues but Q has three. Let the EP:

M $(S_{p\,1x>})$ = p be denoted by ϕ and the EP: M $(S_{q\,1x>})$ = q by ψ. In case (a) we denote EP corresponding to the observable P as ϕ and the EP's corresponding to the observables Q as ψ_1, and ψ_2. When we construct the truth-table 7 for this cases, we find that the truth-table has the following form.

Truth-Table 7

Here we have a surprise: The distributive law has failed: But looking closer, we see that this is expected as the observable P, which has only one eigenvalue, is a constant like the electron charge. Hence the operator P corresponding to this observable is just a number which commutes with every other operator, that is, the observable P is compatible with every other observable. We make a mistake in the first place in taking P with one eigenvalue incompatible with Q.

In the case (b) we denote the EP's corresponding to P as ϕ_1 and ϕ_2 and the EP's corresponding to Q as ψ_1 and ψ_2 In this case we are led to the following truth-table 8.

Truth-Table 8

The truth values in the columns 2 and 8 indicate that the distributive law holds. Finally, in the case (c) we denote the EP's corresponding to P as ϕ_1 and ϕ_2 and the EP's corresponding to Q as ψ_1, ψ_2 and ψ_3 (note that $m \neq n$ here). We construct the following truth table 9.

Truth-Table 9

In this case as well, we see that the distributive law holds, One can easily verify this for more complex cases. From the above truth-tables, we see that the distributive law holds for EP's both in the case of compatible and compatible observables. The apparent failure of the law in the case (2a) is actually the confirmation of its validity.

5. Connective of Negation, Implication and Equivalence:

It can be seen from the above analysis that the distributive law in the form

$$(\lambda_1 V \lambda_2 V....) \Lambda (\mu_1 V \mu_2 V \mu_3....)$$
$$= (\lambda_1 \Lambda \mu_1) V (\lambda_2 \Lambda \mu_2) V (\lambda_3 \Lambda \mu_3).... V (\lambda_j \Lambda \mu_j) V....$$

holds for the EP's corresponding to both compatible and incompatible observables. We have seen that this form, but not the other, is meaningful in our empirical logic within the scope of meaning we have assigned to the connectives of disjunction 'V' and of the conjunction 'Λ'. Another connective we have not mentioned so far and which has a basic function in further development of our logical system is negation '⌉'. If we denote the EP: $M (S_{L1x>}) = l_i$ as λ_j then we shall denote the EP: $M (S_{L1x>}) = \lambda_j$ as $⌉\lambda_j$ we see that the meaning given to the connective of negation is quasi-classical.

Now that we have given empirical meanings to the connectives 'V', 'Λ' and '⌉' we set to define some additional connective like those of implication and equivalence for both compatible and incompatible observables. Our definition of implication happens to provide the same truth-table for it, in these cases as in the classical case: a conditional with a true antecedent and a false consequent is false. This requires that in the case of compatible observables we put $(\alpha \supset \beta_1) \equiv (⌉\alpha V \beta) V (⌉\alpha \Lambda \beta)$ where α and β are the EP's corresponding to the compatible observables A and B. We illustrate this by the following truth-table 10, which can easily be constructed using the above expression on the right

Truth-Table 10

In the case of incompatible observables, we have

$$(\phi \supset \psi) \equiv (⌉\phi V \psi) V ⌉(⌉\phi \Lambda \psi)$$

where ϕ and ψ are the EP's corresponding to the incompatible observables P and Q. This also leads to the same truth-table 10 given above. In the above two expressions we have already used the connective ≡ which is known as that of equivalence. The concept of equivalence in the sense that two EP's (occuring on either side of that connective) are materially equivalent when they have the same truth-value ought to accepted in quantum logic regardless of the nature of EP's as to whether they correspond to compatibles. This requires that if λ and μ are two EP's corresponding to two observables either compatible or incompatible with each other then we put the equivalence relation between as $(\lambda \equiv \mu) \equiv (\lambda \supset \mu) \vee \urcorner(\mu \supset \lambda)$. This holds in both cases. However, in the case of compatible observables with the classical meaning of 'Λ' one may also put $(\alpha \equiv \beta) \equiv (\alpha \supset \beta) \wedge (\beta \supset \alpha)$.

Finally, we present a few consequences of the empirical meanings given to the set of connectives 'V', 'Λ' and ˥. Since experimental meaning have already assigned to these connectives, one need not strive to seek empirical meanings to other connectives defined in terms of these, such as implication and equivalence. Yet it is fruitful briefly investigate the following questions: (1) For which pair of EP's λ, μ the presence of one say λ entails the presence of the other? (2) For which pair of EP's λ and μ the presence of one is entailed by the other? Both questions can be answered within the framework of our logical system, provided we distinguish between two cases of compatible and incompatible observables, (1) If α_i an β_i are the EP's corresponding to two compatible observables A and B, we assert that the presence of α_i (or β_i) entails $(\alpha_i \vee \beta_i) \vee (\alpha_i \wedge \beta_i)$.

Logically this means that $\alpha_i \supset [(\alpha_i \vee \beta_i) \vee (\alpha_i \wedge \beta_i)]$ is a tautology which indeed it is. Empirically it would mean that if α_i is true (or if β_i is true) then $[(\alpha_i \vee \beta_i) \vee (\alpha_i \wedge \beta_i)]$ is true also, but the converse is not true. This can be seen from the following truth-table 11.

Truth Table 11

The above discussion shows that when α_i is true (or when β_i is true), then $\alpha_i \vee \beta_i$ (signifying successive measurements of (A and B) and $\alpha_i \wedge \beta_i$ (which signifies simultaneous measurements of A and B) are two mutually exclusive EP's. Similarly if ϕ_i and ψ_j are the EP's corresponding to two incompatible observables P and Q, we assert that the presence of ϕ_i (∞ y_i) entails the presence of $(\phi_i \vee \psi_j) \vee \neg(\phi_i \wedge \psi_j)$. It is easy to verify that $\phi_i \supset [(\phi_i \vee \psi_j) \vee \neg(\phi_i \wedge \psi_j)]$ is a tautology and that if ϕ_i is true (or if ψ_j is true), then $[(\phi_i \vee \psi_j) \vee \neg(\phi_i \wedge \psi_j)]$ is also true.

Notice the presence of $\neg(\phi_i \wedge \psi_j)$ in the case of incompatible observables instead of $(\phi_i \wedge \psi_j)$. Hence when ϕ_i is true (or when ψ_j is true), then $(\phi_i \vee \psi_j)$ (signifying successive measurements of P and Q) are two mutually exclusive EP's and incomplete.

(2) For compatible observables, one easily verifies that α_i (or β_i) is entailed by $(\alpha_i \wedge \beta_j)$. This means that if $(\alpha_i \wedge \beta_i)$ is true then α_i as well as β_i is true and that $(\alpha_i \wedge \beta_i) \supset \alpha_i$ (or β_i) is a tautology. In similar fashion, one finds that ϕ_i (or ψ_j) is entailed by $\neg(\phi_i \wedge \psi_j)$ where ϕ_i and ψ_j are the EP's for two incompatible observables.

(6) Concluding remarks: We have shown that the basis of logical statements, as is often claimed, is no just a *priori*, but as to take into account empirical truths. A Logic originated and developed during the classical period cannot but be at variance with empirical truths of quantum mechanics developed to explain the behaviour of the microworld. If logic is claimed to be empirical, is it merely dropping a well-known law of classical logic and nothing else? We answer this question by saying that it is much more. If the logic is empirical, then one must investigate the empirical meanings of the basic connectives like those of disunjtion and conjunction in the light of new insights two measurement processes of the microworld. Do the classical meanings of these connectives, which have been

time- tested in the classical context, remain unscathed when we look beyond the classical world and peep into the microworld of atoms, nuclie and elementary particles or do they undergo any change? Our investigation has shown that we have to adopt the latter alternative. In this process we find that we have to distinguish between compatible and incompatible observables of quantum mechanics and adopt two different deviant logics for these cases.

Appendix I

In this appendix we present two truth-tables 12 and 13 for EP' corresponding to compatible and incompatible observables respectively and list the laws in formal logic which hold and which do not hold in our deviant logics.

[Truth Table (12) & Truth Table (13)]

In the above table, the disjunction 'V' is an exclusive disjunction. The negation and conjunction happen to coincide with their classical counterparts, so do the implemation and equivalence. We have expressed the implication in terms of the above connectives of negation, disjunction and conjunction as $(\alpha \supset \beta) \equiv (\urcorner\alpha \vee \beta) \vee (\urcorner\alpha \wedge \beta)$

We express the equivalence $(\alpha \equiv \beta)$ as either $(\alpha \supset \beta) \vee \urcorner(\beta \supset \alpha)$ or $(\alpha \supset \beta) \wedge (\beta \supset \alpha)$

Using the above truth-table 12, one may easily verify the following;

(1) $(\alpha \vee \urcorner\alpha)$ is a tautology, (1) $(\alpha \wedge \urcorner\alpha)$ is a contradiction, (3) Modus ponens holds, (4) Modus Tollens holds, (5) Disjunctive Syllogism holds, (6) Hypothetical Syllogism holds, (7) Addition fails, (8) Simplification holds, (9) Conjunction holds (10) Communication holds, (11) Association holds, (12) De Mogan's Law fails and finally (13) Double Negation holds.

In the above table, negation is classical, disjunction is exclusive and conjunction happens to be the negation of the classical counterpart. The implication is expressed as $(\phi \supset \psi) \equiv (\rceil\phi \vee \psi) \vee \rceil(\rceil\phi \wedge \psi)$ and the equivalence is expressed as $(\phi \supset \psi) \vee \rceil(\psi \supset \phi)$. Again using the above truth-table 13 one may verify the following: (1) $(\phi \vee \rceil\phi)$ is a tautology, (2) $\rceil(\phi \wedge \rceil\phi)$ is a contradiction, (3) Modus Ponens holds, (4) Modus Tollens holds, (5) Disjunctive Syllogism holds, (6) Hypothecatival Syllogism holds, (7) Addition fails, (8) simplification fails, (9) Conjunction fails, (10) Commutation holds, (11) Association holds for 'V' but fails for 'Λ' (12) De Morgans' Law fails, finally (13) Double Negation holds.

Appendix II

Adequate system of Connectives: It is shown in the works on logicc that the set of classical connectives $\rceil$, V_{cl} and Λ_{cl} is adequate to express any truth-function. Since the exclusive disjunction 'V' we have introduced in our logical system can be expressed in terms of the above set, in the form

$(\alpha \vee \beta) \equiv (\alpha \vee_{cl} \beta) \wedge_{dl} \rceil(\alpha \wedge_{cl} \beta)$, the set , V and 'Λ' of our deviant logic for compatible observables is adequate.

In the case of incompatible observables as well, the set $\rceil$, 'V' and 'Λ' is also adequate to express any truth-function in this case, as the conjunction 'Λ' used in our logical system is seen from the truth-tables 12 and 13 to be the negation of the classical conjunction 'Λ_{cl}'. Hence a well-formed formula (wff) of the type $\rceil\phi \vee (\psi \wedge \chi)$ for EP's corresponding to incompatible observables can be expressed in terms of ' $\rceil$'. 'V_l 'Λ_{cl}' and as follows:

$$\rceil\phi \vee (\psi \wedge \chi)$$
$$\equiv [\rceil\phi \vee_{cl} (\psi \wedge \chi)] \wedge_{cl} \rceil[\rceil\phi \wedge_{cl} (\psi \wedge \chi)]$$
$$\equiv [\rceil\phi \vee_{cl} \rceil(\psi \wedge \chi)] \wedge_{cl} \rceil(\rceil\phi \wedge_{cl} \rceil(\psi \wedge_{cl} \chi))$$

Truth Table 1

α	β	$\alpha \vee \beta$
T	T	F
T	F	T
F	T	T
F	F	F

Truth Table 2

α_i	β_i	$\alpha_i \wedge \beta_i$
T	T	T
T	F	F
F	T	F
F	F	F

Truth Table 3

ϕ_i	ψ_i	$\phi_i \wedge \psi_i$
T	T	F
T	F	T
F	T	T
F	F	T

Truth Table 4

α	$\wedge$	β_1	$\vee$	β_2	$\alpha \wedge \beta_1$	$\vee$	$\alpha \wedge \beta_2$
T	T	T	T	F	T	T	F
F	F	T	T	F	F	F	F
T	T	F	T	T	F	T	T
F	F	F	T	T	F	F	F

Truth Table 5

$(\alpha_1$	V	$\alpha_2)$	Λ	$(\beta_1$	V	$\beta_2)$	$\alpha_1 \Lambda \beta_1$	$\alpha_1 \Lambda \beta_2$	$\alpha_2 \Lambda \beta_1$	$\alpha_2 \Lambda \beta_2$	V
T	T	F	T	T	T	F	T	F	F	F	T
T	T	F	T	F	T	T	F	T	F	F	T
F	T	T	T	T	T	F	F	F	T	F	T
F	T	T	T	F	T	T	F	F	F	T	T

Truth Table 6

α_1	α_2	α_3	β_1	β_2	β_3	$(\alpha_1 \vee \alpha_2 \vee \alpha_3)$	$\wedge$	$(\beta_1 \vee \beta_2 \vee \beta_3)$	$\alpha_1 \wedge \beta_1$
T	F	F	T	F	F	T	T	T	T
T	F	F	F	T	F	T	T	T	F
T	F	F	F	F	T	T	T	T	F
F	T	F	T	F	F	T	T	T	F
F	T	F	F	T	F	T	T	T	F
F	T	F	F	F	T	T	T	T	F
F	F	T	F	F	F	T	T	T	F
F	F	T	F	T	F	T	T	T	F
F	F	T	F	F	T	T	T	T	F

$\alpha_1 \wedge \beta_2$	$\alpha_1 \wedge \beta_2$	$\alpha_2 \wedge \beta_1$	$\alpha_3 \wedge \beta_2$	$\alpha_2 \wedge \beta_3$	$\alpha_2 \wedge \beta_1$	$\alpha_3 \wedge \beta_2$	$\alpha_3 \wedge \beta_3$	V
F	F	F	F	F	F	F	F	T
T	F	F	F	F	F	F	F	T
F	T	F	F	F	F	F	F	T
F	F	T	F	F	F	F	F	T
F	F	F	T	F	F	F	F	T
F	F	F	F	T	F	F	F	T
F	F	F	F	F	T	F	F	T
F	F	F	F	F	F	T	F	T
F	F	F	F	F	F	F	T	T

Truth Table 7

ϕ	Λ	Ψ_1	Λ	Ψ_2	$\phi \Lambda \Psi_1$	$\phi \Lambda \Psi_2$	V
T	F	T	T	F	F	T	T
F	T	T	T	F	T	T	F
T	T	F	T	T	T	F	T
F	T	F	T	T	T	T	F

Truth Table 8

ϕ_1	V	ϕ_2	Λ	Ψ_1	V	Ψ	$\phi_1 \Lambda \Psi_1$	$\phi_2 \Lambda \Psi_1$	$\phi_2 \Lambda \Psi_1$	$\phi_2 \Lambda \Psi_2$	V
T	T	F	F	T	T	F	F	T	T	T	F
T	T	F	F	F	T	T	T	F	T	T	F
F	T	T	F	T	T	F	T	T	F	T	F
F	T	T	F	F	T	T	T	T	T	F	F

Truth Table 9

ϕ_1	ϕ_2	ψ_1	ψ_2	ψ_3	$\phi_1 V \phi_2$	$\psi_1 V \psi_2 V \psi_3$	Λ	$\phi_1 \Lambda \psi_1$	$\phi_1 \Lambda \psi_2$	$\phi_1 \Lambda \psi_3$	$\phi_2 \Lambda \psi_1$	$\phi_2 \Lambda \psi_2$	$\phi_3 \Lambda \psi_3$	V
T	F	T	F	F	T	T	F	F	T	T	T	T	T	F
F	T	T	F	F	T	T	F	T	T	T	F	T	T	F
T	F	F	T	F	T	T	F	T	F	T	T	T	T	F
F	T	F	T	F	T	T	F	T	T	T	F	F	T	F
T	F	F	F	T	T	T	T	T	F	T	T	T	T	F
F	T	F	F	T	T	T	F	T	T	T	T	T	F	F

Truth Table 10

α	β	$\alpha \supset \beta$
T	T	T
T	F	F
F	T	T
F	F	T

Truth Table 11

α_1	β_1	$\alpha_1 \vee \beta_1$	$\alpha_1 \wedge \beta_1$	$(\alpha_1 \vee \beta_1) \vee (\alpha_1 \wedge \beta_1)$
T	T	F	T	T
T	F	T	F	T
F	T	T	F	T

Truth Table 12

α	β	¬α	¬β	α ∨ β	α ∧ β	α ⊃ β	β ⊃ α	α ≡ β
T	T	F	F	F	T	T	T	T
T	F	F	T	T	F	F	T	F
F	T	T	F	T	F	T	F	F
F	F	T	T	F	F	T	T	T

Truth Table 13

φ	ψ	¬φ	¬ψ	φ ∨ ψ	φ ∧ ψ	φ ⊃ ψ	ψ ⊃ φ	φ ≡ ψ
T	T	F	F	F	F	T	T	T
T	F	F	T	T	T	F	T	F
F	T	T	F	T	T	T	F	F
F	F	T	T	F	T	T	T	T

Chapter IV

Role of Universals, Thought Experiments: *Reductio ad Absurdum*

In this Chapter we have a general survey of space-time and other aspects of varied ideas connecting with them.

The following are listed below:

Section (a) Role of Universals

Section (b) Thought Experiments

Section (c) *Reductio ad Absurdum.*

In section (a) we try re-define Universals as a relational aspect resulting as a unification of space-time.

In Section (b) this is mainly to discuss the status of time. In thought Experiments (Gedanken). The temporal points as that the 'Now' of the metaphysicians is also discussed.

In Section (c) discussed mainly as the '*Reductio ad Absurdum* as the dialectic of Nagarjuna of the ancient schools. The modern views are correlated with my thought of Heterologic which is sufficiently discussed in the last chapter.

Section A

Redefining Universals

In this section, we try to re-define Universals* as a relation aspect between space and time.

Before, we begin that let us observe some views of eminent personalities who in general, remark about universals.

---

* Redefining Univerrsals' Indian Philosophical Quarterly Vol. IX No. 3, April 1982 - Filita Bharucha (This article has been included in `World Philosopher Index')

For example the words of Arthur Eddington says : It is not at all necessary that every individual symbol that is used should represent something in common experience or even something explicable to common experience". So in general, I also think that atleast a total mathematical symbol cannot be used to describe universal. Russell considers the class of universals as the class of relations. This helps us to create a spatio-temporal relation. It further maintains the ideas of Logico-Hetero-spatio-temporal continuum.

There are many view points of several thinkers regarding universals. I also consider the class of universals as the class of relations, so I have also made a "logical construct" of equivalence relations regarding universals in general. However let us now discuss the view-point of universals in context of binary relation of space and time.

As we know that space and time are limitness extension. Undoubtedly objective and subject view-points have been opined by various philosophers regarding space and time. Questions like:

"What is time" when actually a foreigner `Means' to ask the question `what is the time'

Coming back to our discussion of the binary relation of space and time, we notice that most ancient philosophers have considered space (*Akasa*) and Time (*Kala*) as a binary relation.

However, I think that Jaines by their Syadvada theory have brought them together in somewhat unary way.

In the 20th century, Einsteins unification of apace and time have been justified. This unificati‿n of space and time has been utilised for understanding of physical theories and made a ground for microscopic fields. However this make 'Universals' a spatio-temporal binary relation.

In the last Chapter of this work, the "Logico-spatio Temporal' has brought out a continuum by Logical Manifolds.

Section B

Status of 'Time' in Thought Experiments

Let we discuss the status of time in view thought experiments called Gedanken Etymologically the German word 'Gedanke" arose from the literal translation of 'thought processes'. Hence a 'Gedanken was supposed to be phenomena (o experiment) carried out only in thought processes of the human mind. Hence I shall in order to abbreviate, use the symbol (G.E), for 'thought experiments' and N (G.E), for the empirically verifiable ones.

In order to understand the problem of (Gedanke Experiment) (GE) in philosophy (metaphysical) one can take up various issues like (1) Belief in intelligibility uniformity of nature.

The status of temporal becoming is a typical philosophical problems. Some meta-physicians have insisted on the time flow' because they believe in a given instant of time namely that the 'Now' is momentarily 'alive' and is much more real than other temporal points of events that are in the distant future keep moving towards the 'Now until they coincide with it and subsequently recede further and further into the past. The complication is due to the fact that the constraints placed on the specific methodological device in metaphysics are not so rigidly attached as in science. Also we note that thought experiments (G.E) cannot provide new empirical data they nevertheless have basically the same function felt we note that (G.E) gives the scientist access to information which is simultaneously at hand and yet inaccessible to him (G.E) helps scientist to draw hidden implications of the same which helps in reconceptualised leading to a scientific revolt.

Before we begin our discussion of (GE) in metaphysics with respect to the temporal becoming, let us discuss the view of time, which human beings in widely different cultural settings and various periods of history have regarded as one of the most central features of existence. That time moves so that events are carried from the future towards us and then recede further into the past. The above case be considered to ancient view of time (t). However, we note that the majority of philosophers e.g. Russell to not agree with transient view of time. They feel that all events and moments stay for ever fixed in position (space) by the framework which they occur. The does not exist an entity as the moving "Now". Time remains still and all temporal relations are permanent., This perhaps was due to Russell's suggestion that one can achieve greater anthological enonomy (Ockhns razor) by eliminating all transient features of time. Still one is able to talk of temporal experiences.

However Russell's view on transient view have been accepted by philosophers like J.J.C. Smart, Mc Taggart who articulated the deeply entrenched common sense view to which temporal points from the fortune, together with events that accounted for those points keep approaching the "Now" of "Apna" momentarily coinciding with it keep on receding into the past. Hence in the next section I shall discuss "A Thought experiment in metaphysics" to context of the above mentioned controversy of transient view of time.

In this case we consider briefly an imaginary situation. Let us suppose that our knowledge of physics of astronomy is considerably greater then it actually is and that on the basis of solar radiation, we establish that our solar system is in years old. Let us suppose that our knowledge of physics of astronomy is considerably greater then it actually is and that on the basis of solar radiation, we establish that our solar system is in yeas old. Let us assume that this year we discover the existence of another solar system say X, many billion of light years satisfying following conditions:

(I) The same initial/conditions prevail as in our system

(II) The same laws of nature prevail.

Suppose we can communicate with the people of planet X by instantaneous signals. We are told by the people of x that the age of their solar system x is (n-300) years old. According to the following report of the state of their planet and the state of their whole solar system, we find that their description fits the state of our own planet and the rest of our solar system in the year say 1691. The most remarkable feature of X turns out to be that its time is passing twice as quickly as ours and thus when we celebrate the beginning of 1982 they will have already reached 1683 and when we are commemorating the 10th anniversary of our first verbal contact with X they are celebrating the 20th anniversary of some century.

This (GE) experiment will of course confront difficulties due to Russell and Stand-point (views) but we introduced it to understand how flow of time can effect (GE), perhaps not (GE). Can we conclude that (GE) and N(GE) are discontinuous functions of time.

Section C

Reductio ad Absurdum

The advent of the 20th century ventures into ancient thinking which could visualize modern ideas of Modern logic. Actually modern logic in the last part of this 20th century has concentrated on formalizing the language of 'symbolic logic' which has used for computers and electronics. I myself have developed a different view of 'Hetero-logic' which can used of Quantum Theories. This is going to be discussed in the last chapter.

Meanwhile at the moment I am going to push forward the ancient schools of thinking mainly' The Dialetic of the (famous Buddhist philosopher) Nagarjuna'

To push forward his philosophy like other dialectians of the world, Nagarjuna has used the famous *"reductio ad absurdum"* (*Prasangapadanam*).

By this he proves the absurdity of his opponents this is and he rejects the 4 possibilities of every concept.

(i) is (ii) is-not (iii) and is not (iv) 'is' nor 'is-not'.

In other words the *Madhyamika* dialectic proceeds as follows.

They classify all views on any problem to be formulated under 4 classes.

(a) affirmative (*sat*)

(b) negative (*asat*)

(c) conjunctive assertion of both (*ubhaya*)

(d) disjunctive denial (*anabharaya*)

Every view reveals inherent contradictions and hence is rejected. However the rejection of one view does not mean the acceptance of the opposite view.

Example of the use of the dialectic to important categories like causality, motion and rest, modes and substance (*atman*) are amply illustrated.

Below I have considered Nagarjuna's use of the dialetic in order to be able to grasp the rue meaning of *sunyata.*

The meaning of sunyata has ways of describing it. I selected one of the definition from Sthiramati's *Madhyanata-vibhangatika* as follows:

Suchness, reality limit, the signless, the ultimate reality- the element of *dharma.*

The following 4 folds with two truths in each have been formulated.

First fold

(a) Existence is the conventional truth

(b) Sunyata is the transcendental truth

Second fold

(a) The first fold of the two truths is the conventional truth.

(b) Neither existence nor sunyata is the transcendental truth.

Third fold

(a) the third fold of these two truths is the conventional truth

(b) Neither existence no non-sunyata is the transcendental truth.

Fourth fold

(a) The third fold of these two truths is the conventional truth.

(b) Neither not one-existence nor not non-sunyata is the transcendental truth.

Hence we see these negative explanations are necessary to lead as to the ideal state.

The two truths of the four folds indicate the middle path i.e. to have refuted every kind of extreme view.

It is theory of "Eight Noes".

No annihilation,	No production
No destruction,	No persistence
No unity,	No plurality
No coming in,	No going out

According to the *Madhyamika* School every kind of extreme view can be refuted by these eight noes.

However since the reader is likely to misunderstand the above it is important to clarify the following points.

(1) The dialectic is not itself a view-point or a synthesis of various view-points. It is only a criticism.

(2) Rejection of all thought categories and views is the rejection of the competence of Reason, to apprehend reality. The real is transcendent to thought, it is thought, it is nondual (sunya), free from all duality of 'is' and is-not'.

(3) All knowledge whether perceptual or inferred is relative and there is none that is absolute true. Nagarjuna

accordingly does not believe in outer reality nor in the inner and his doctrine is therefore described as that of the void (Sunya-Vada).

(4) His method of dichotomy bears a resemblance to that method used by Bradley in modern times. By these use of this method he tries to show how the common concepts of philosophy are self-discrepant and are nothing more than dogmatic assumption.

(5) In more than one chapter of his 'Karika', Nagarjuna passes in view, conceptions like 'motion' showing how they are utterly unintelligible.

(6) The catharsis of modern psychology can be compared the dialectic which is merely a process of purification of intellect.

Chapter V

General Theories of Space Time

This Chapter deals with a general brief survey of various views regarding space and time which have observed not only by philosophers, physicists but also the so-called common dassein (human).

However, before we discuss the Einstein's Space-time four- dimensional manifold in favour of the unification of space and time characteristic of the relativity theory; we shall begin with the origin of the Absolute-Relational controversy.

Newton* on absolute space and time is making atleast four interrelated but distinct claims as follows:-

(i) Absolute Motion : Space and time are capable to support a non-relational absolute motion.

(ii) Immutabily:-The structures fixed and immutable

(iii) Nonconventional:- The structures are intrinsic to space and time.

(iv) Substantivalism:- Structure inhere in a substratum of space or space-points.

We note that Newton has used to terms 'time', 'space', 'place',and 'motion' not in their ordinary-language senses but are being given special technical meanings that are being explained as follows :

(i) Newton says that absolute time "flows equably" he is not to be passed as saying that time flows and that it flows equally. A literal notion of flows would presuppose a substratum with respect to which the flow takes *place*.

---

* Newton's Scholium on *Absolute Space and Time* reproduced as an Appendix to this chapter.

(ii) Saying that time flows equally "without relation to anything to external". Newton is asserting that the temporal internal between two events as what it is *independent of bodies* are in space and how they behave.

(iii) Thirdly, Newton is distinguishing true mathematical time from sensible and external measure of it. He is asserting that the *metric of time* is intrinsic to temporal intervals and that talk about the lapse of time between and is not elliptical for talk about the relation of and to the behaviour of a pendulum or any other physical system.

(iv) "*Absolute space* in its own nature without relation to anything external remains always similar and immovable", this is structure of space being absolute as maintained by Newton. This *immovable structure* was assumed to be that of the Euclidean three-space E'. place is part of the space which a body which a body which takes up and is according to the space either absolute or relation.

We summarise the senses of Absoluteness as follows:

(1) Space-time is endowed with various structures that are intrinsic to it.

(2) Among these structures are absolute simultaneity (i.e. a unique partition of events into simultaneity classes) and an absolute duration (i.e. a measure of temporal lapse that is independent of the path connecting the events).

(3) Thee is an absolute reference frame that provides a unique way of identifying spatial locations through time. As a result, there is an absolute or well-defined measure of the velocity of individual particles and a well defined measure of spatial separation for any pair of events.

(4) The structure of space-time is immutable i.e. it is the same from time to time in the actual world and from this world do other physically possible worlds.

(5) Space-time is substance in that it forms a substratum that underlies physical events and processes, and spatiotemporal relations among such events and processes are parasitic on the spatiotemporal relations inherent in the substratum of space-time points and regions.

Now we begin dealing with the aspect of *Relationism.*

(1) There are two reasons why relationism is a more elusive doctrine than absolutism. First, there is no relationist counterpart to Newton's Scholium, the locus classicus of absolutism.

(2) At the risk of some distortion it is nevertheless useful to state three themes that form the core of classical relationism. The first theme is about both the nature of motion and the structure of space-time. All motion is the relative motion of bodies, and consequently, space-time does not have, and cannot have, structures that support absolute quantities of motion.

(3) The second theme is a denial of space-time substantivalism. Spatiotemporal relations among bodies and evens are direct, that is, they are not parasitic on relations among substratum of space points that underlie bodies or space-time points that underlie events.

(4) The third theme asserts that all spatial predication is relational in nature. No irreducible, monadic spatiotemporal properties, like is located at space-time point p', appear in a correct analysis of the spatiotemporal idiom.

Apart after dealing with the controversy between Absolute and Relational Groups, I cannot ignore the greats mathematician Leibniz with his idealist view attacking the absolute space. For the believed that space and time are not fully real; that they are 'IDEAL'. It is true that in the Leibnizian metaphysic what are their monerelational properties and what we call the physical world is not an appearance or phenomenon.

It is not possible to discuss all the Classical Space-time theories in that book, however, we mention some of them.

(a) Leibnizian Space-Time which I have all the Classical Space-Time Theories in that book, however, we mention some of them.

(b) Neo-Newtonian or Galilean Space-Time } Mainly in effect of particular inertial frame

(c) Aristotelian Space-Time.

(d) Machian Space-Time.

(e) Maxwellian Space-Time.

I summarize these Classical Space-Time Theories in a Table:

Sn.	*Name*	*Structures*	*Symmetries*	*Invariants*
1.	Machian Space-time	Absolute simultaniety Structure of the instantaneous spaces.	$X \to x^{1/\alpha} = R^{\alpha}_{\beta}(t) + a^{\alpha}(t)$ $t \to t^{2} = f(t),\ df/dt > 0$	Relative particle distances
2.	Leibnizian Space-time	(1) + time metric	$x \to x^{1/\alpha} = R^{\alpha}_{\beta}(t)x^{\beta} + a^{\alpha}(t)$ $t \to t' = t + \text{const}$	Relative particle velocities, accelerations, etc.
3.	Maxwellian Space-time	(2) + standard of rotation	$t \to t' = t + \text{const}$ $x \to x' = R^{\alpha}_{\beta}x^{\beta} + a^{\alpha}(t)$	Rotation for an extended body.
4.	Neo-Newtonian Space-time	(3) + inertial structure	$t \to t' = t + \text{const.}$ $x \to x' = R^{\alpha}_{\beta}x^{\beta} + v^{\alpha}(t) + \text{const.}$	Acceleration of a particle
5.	Full Newtonian Space-time	(4) + absolute space	$x \to x' = R^{\alpha}_{\beta}x^{\beta} + \text{const.}$ $t \to t' = t + \text{const.}$	Velocity of a particle
6.	Aristotelian Space-time	(5) + distinguished spatial origin	$t \to t' = t + \text{const.}$ $x \to x' = R^{\alpha}_{\beta}x^{\beta}$	Distance from the center of the universe

Note: $R^{a}_{b}(t)$ is a time dependent orthonogal matrix.
$a^{\alpha}(t)$ are arbitrary smooth functions of time.

Clearing up the discussion about the classical Space-time theories we come to the perspective on Einsten's geometrical interpretation of 1908. On this interpretation of the Special Theory of relativity describes a four-dimensional semi-Euclidean manifold, with the line element given by.

$$ds^2 = dx_0^2 - dx_1^2 - dx_2^2 - dx_3^2$$

The inertial frames are just the Cartesian co-ordinates systems for this line element and the Lorentz transformations are analogous to the Euclidean orthogonal transformations. The trajectories or world-lines of free particles are straight lines or geodesics of the metric (1) they are four-dimensional curves of extreme in fact maximal-Length according to ds and which they satisfy the linear equation $x_i = a_i u + b_i$ in all inertial frames.

There is indeed no three-dimensional Euclidean embedding space but there is a four-dimensional semi-Euclidean space-time in which all physical events, are embedding. Within this space-time manifold, a privileged class of straight lines or inertial trajectiones represents the world-lines of free particles. Once again we start the flat Minkowski manifold with the line element given as above earlier.

$$\text{(I)} \qquad ds^2 = dx_0^2 - dx_1^2 - dx_2^2 - dx_3^2$$

for which we impart a variable curvature to this manifold, where the degree of curvature in a given region depends on the distribution of mass and energy, since our new manifold is not flat or semi-Euclidean we can no longer use the simple for (1) for the line element, but we need the general form.

$$ds^2 = \sum_{i,j=0}^{3} g_{ij}\, dx_i\, dx_j \text{ where } g_{ij}\text{'s are not constant.}$$

but are the new metric intercept as world lines of possibly free falling (gravitationally affected) particles.

The most important aim of our space timer theories is to *describe* the trajectorics of physical particles, free particles, or particles affected by gravitational force or charged particles subject to an electromagnetic field. We represents a trajectory by a curve in space-time a continuous and differentiable map from an interval of the real line into out manifold.

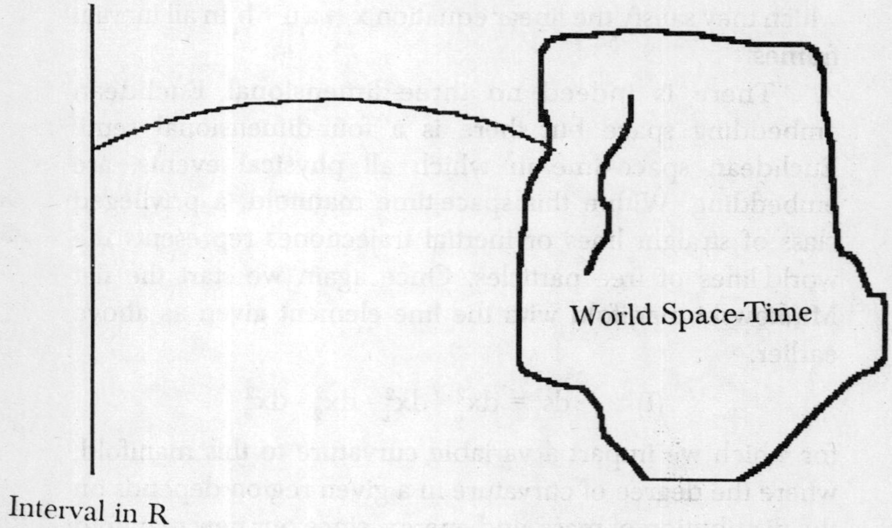

We call curves 'World-lines' in space-time.

In the next section we shall have the co-ordination of space-Time as a four-dimensional differentiable manifold with its properties.

Co-ordinatization of Space-Time:

Space-Time is a four-dimensional differentible manifold.

Let us characterise its properties.

(1) Firstly it is a topology having a point in space-time with a neighbour say M.

(ii) Secondly space-time is co-ordinatizable by R^4 i.e. set of four (Quadruplex) real numbers.

(iii) Thirdly we define one-one continuous function from the neighbour M to R^4 that is illustrated by

(iv) Consider a real-valued function defined on a neighbourhood in space-time. *Then* we can say is differentiable only if (i.e. apply – the inverse of g) then it is differentiable from into R for *every* function g.)

Space-Time

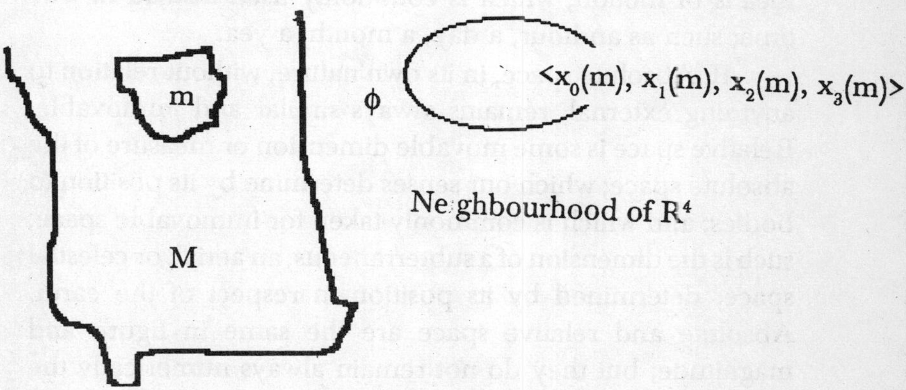

Co-ordination of Space-Time

(v) Space-Time is a four-dimensional differentiable is purely *LOCAL ASSERTION.*

Appendix

Newton's Scholium on *Absolute Space and Time*

Hitherto I have laid down the definition of such words as are less known, and explained the sense in which I would have them to be understood in the following discourse. I do not define time, space, place, and motion, as being well known to all. Only I must observe, that the common people conceive those quantities under no other notions but from the relation they bear to sensible objects. And thence arise certain prejudices, for the removing of which it will be convenient to distinguish them into absolute and relative, true and apparent, mathematical and common.

I. Absolute, true, and mathematical time, of itself, and from its own nature, flows equably without relation to anything external, and by another name is called duration; relative, apparent and comment time, is some sensible and external (whether accurate or unequable) measure of duration by the means of motion, which is commonly used instead of true time; such as an hour, a day, a month, a yea.

II. Absolute space, in its own nature, without relation to anything external, remains always similar and immovable. Relative space is some movable dimension or measure of the absolute space; which our senses determine by its position to bodies; and which is commonly taken for immovable space; such is the dimension of a subterraneous, an aerial, or celestial space, determined by its position in respect of the earth. Absolute and relative space are the same in figure and magnitude; but they do not remain always numerically the same. For if the earth, for instance, moves, a space of our air, which relatively and in respect of the earth remains always the same., will at one time be one part of the absolute space into which the air passes; at another time it will be another part of the same, and so, absolutely understood, it will be continually changed.

III. Place is a part of space which a body takes up, and is according to the space, either absolute or relative. I say, a part of space; not the situation, nor the external surface of the body. For the places of equal solids are always equal but their surfaces, by reason of their dissimilar figures, are often unequal. Positions properly have no quantity, nor are they so much the places themselves, as the properties of places. The motion of the whole is the same with the sum of the motions of the parts; that is, the translation of the whole, out of its place, is the same thing with the sum of the translations of the parts out of their places; and therefore the place of the whole is the same as the sum of the places as the parts, and for that reason, it is internal, and in the whole body.

IV. Absolute motion is the translation of a body from one absolute place into another; and relative motion, the translation from one relative place into another. Thus in a ship under sail, the relative place of a body is that part of the ship which the body possesses; or that part of the cavity which the body fills, and which therefore moves together with the ship; and relative rest is the continuance of the body in the same part of the ship, of its cavity. But real, absolute rest, is the continuance of the body in the same part of that immovable space, in which the ship itself, its cavity, and all that it contains, is moved. Wherefore, if the earth is really at rest, the body, which relatively rests in the ship, will really and absolutely move with the same velocity which the ship has on the earth. But if the earth also moves, the true and absolute motion of the body will arise, partly from the true motion of the earth, in immovable space, partly from the relative motion of the ship on the earth; and if the body moves also relatively in the ship, its true motion will arise, partly from the true motion of the earth, in immovable space, and partly from the relative motions as well of the ship on the earth, as of the body in the ship, and from these relative motions will arise the relative motion of the body on the earth. As if that part of the earth, where the ship is, was truly moved towards the east, with a velocity of 10001 parts; while the ship itself, with a fresh gale and full sails, is carried towards the west, with a velocity expressed by 10 of those parts; but a sailor walks in the ship towards the east, with 1 pat of the said velocity; then the sailor will be moved truly in immovable space towards the east, with a velocity of 10001 parts, and relatively on the earth towards the west, with a velocity of 9 of those parts.

Chapter VI

Logico-Spatio-Temporal Space*

This is the Chapter that I read in Berlin (July 1992) and contains some thoughts of space-time regarding physical events in an empirical stand point with my Hetero-Logical angle. This is done after considering the earlier chapters containing similar thoughts of the Jainas ancient school and empirical modern view-points.

Actually the Hetero-Logical should be accompanied by two divisions (a) probability dealing with the physical sciences (b) possibility dealing with the Social Sciences. However in respect of the embroyonic stage in my Heterologic. I select the (a) Probability section for this book at the moment. A forecast of another book containing the other division is seen.

The last section in this paper of book contains matrix formulation and also a geometrical structure of it.

Lastly this chapter containing my ideas should be developed in the advance of the microscopic field, which I hope to do in future.

Logic-Spatio-Temporal Space

Abstract:-

In this paper, I want to show how we materialise physical 'events' in the concept of space-time continuum. A logical construct considered to define physical events $(E_j)\, j \geq 1$ in $[(R^3 \times T) \times L^n_m]$** which that determines with reference to a system S.

---

* Paper presented in Berlin, Germany.

** $[(R^3 \times T) \times L^n_m]$ the semi-Riemannion Manifold can also be considered as a "Logico-Spatio-Temporal Manifold" (See Appendix I).

$$^{+}[(R^3 \times T) \times L^n_m] = \{[(x,y,z); t]; (n,m)\}$$

for

$$(x,y,z) \in R^3, \quad t \in T, \quad (n,m) \in L^n_m$$

where $\in$ denotes to the value 'belongs to'.

The values of n, m are discussed in the "Heterologic Approach" as follows:

As we know that '*physical events*' depend on a *space-time-Continuum* which is represented by some relational system based of activity in the *Physical* world which is transcient and fluctuation.

For this, we introduce a 'Hetero-Logical Approach" which evaluates the concepts of *events*. In Heterological Approach, we *only* consider *truth-values* (T.V.) depend on concept of probability i.e. their supremum[++] of truth-values that in turn depends of supremum of probability.

We begin the Hetero-Logic Approach which is required by the space $[(R^3 \times T) \times L^n_m$

The "Heterologic Approach" :

I. Outline below in brief some of the developments as follows:

Assumption: Our "system S" has its own logic L of respective degree and order.

Definition I: The number of different truth-values (T.V.) that a proposition P can take is defined as *Order* of Logic L.

e.g. on N-valued logic has order n where 'n' natural numbers. In the case of discussion "events" today, *we consider order 2.*

Definition II: To determine the degree of a logic L, we can proceed as follows:

\+ Ref to Appendix I of this Chapter VI.

++ Ref to Appendix II of this Chapter VI.

Let P_1 denote the probability $0 \leq P_i \leq 1$ of *occurrence truth-value* T_1 (in a ***particulars truth-table***).

For any well-formed (formula (w.f.f.)) A, define the degree as A as

$$d(A) = \text{Supremum } (p_i / i \in \text{truth-values})$$

as well as

$$\text{Infirmum } (p_i / i \in \text{truth-values})$$

where $\in$ denotes "belongs to"

Then, we define the *degree of a Logic L* as follows:

$$d(L) = \text{Supremum } (d(A)/\text{for all } A) = m_1 \text{ (say)}$$

as well as

$$\text{Infirmum } (d(A) / \text{for all } A) = m_2 \text{ (say)}$$

with the above definitions of order and degree of a logic L, we shall denote a logic of order n and degree m as L^n_m where n, natural number, $m = (m_1, m_2)$

Footnote: In the case of materialising events we have the *supremum* of the degree. In our context every space and time constitue a relational system expressing certain General Features of the Physical objects and they are descriptions of the physical world.

Note I: The hierarchy of truth-values (T.V.) with reference to order and degree of logic is strictly for numerical convenience and has no ethical importance.

Note II: An axiomatic system has a constant degree each probabilities have same truth-values viz. same probability i.e., either probability one (1) corresponding to truth-value True (T) or probability zero (0) corresponding to truth-value False (F).

Note III: A methogenic system has varying degrees. I would consider mathematics to be an axiomatic system, certain probabilities are rejects or acceptance only on the basis of inconsistency of assumption whereas most of the fields involve methodogenic systems e.g. we saw in the physics though both the retarded and advanced solutions are mathematically consistent though we only accept the retarded ones as they agree with the experimental (methodogenical) evidences as far.

Definition III: "*Logical constants*" are entities with a formal character i.e. which remains constant under changing conditions of a system. In particular `logical entities' are spatio-temporal constants.

Definition IV: An entity that is not a logical constant we shall call *existential* i.e. entity that changes with the changing conditions of a system, It is only when we intercept an *existential entity* as a logical entity fallacy arises. Vagueness is not clear when a particular statement is placed in a logic of inaccurate degree and order and the conclusion is inappropriate. Hence, the best remedy to avoid vagueness is the appropriate classification of a statement to its particular logic. If conditions change and we are able to determine the order and degree then the non-denotational phrase will have a reference. A proposition P subject to conditions C_1, C_2, C_3. C_n may to logic 'L' of degree d_1 (say) and may change its *logical status* to logic 'L' of degree d_2 (say). Therefore the degree of a logic to which a proposition belongs determine the logical status of that proposition.

Definition V: A proposition is *incorrect* if it is not classified under a logic of *appropriate degree.*

Definition VI: A proposition is *inconclusive* if it is not classified under a logic of *appropriate order.*

Definition VII: The proposition P_1, P_2 are *comparable* (equivalent to unto language isomorphism) if they belong to logic L with the *same order.*

Definition VIII: Two proposition P_1, P_2 are absolutely *comparable* (complete equivalence) if they belong to logic L with the *same order* and *degree.*

The exact determination of the order and degree at present may appear difficult to evaluate in certain fields due to the construction of a *specific-truth-table*. However, one can for example in quantum mechanics use analyses o fitters and the idea of a *maximum observable set to determine them.*

Summarising so far, we see that with respect to a system S one can have L_m^n (i.e. a logic 'L' of order n degree M)

As we notice by the earlier section, a reference of an event expressed as a proposition does not determine "truth" or "falsehood" (or any truth-values as such) it merely enables to ascertain order and degree of its corresponding logic.

Now we represent an event E with a matrix having space-time co-ordinates and order, degree forms as follows:

Matrix Formulation of Events (E_i) of the Dual Manifold (R^4, $L^2_{(0,1)}$)

R^4 : Space-time manifold

L^N_M : Logico-Manifold where N = 2 (Order)

M = (m_1, m_2) = (0,1) (degree)

Space Time Points $X_i \neq \{(2_i, y_i, z_i)\} = (r_i, t_i)$ E R^4

Propositions Y_i $L^2_{(0,1)}$ (Logico-Manifold with Order 2.)

degree (m_1 m_2) = (0_i 1).

A_i is a well formed formula corresponding to the propositions Y_i where degree $(A_i) \in L_{(0,1)}$ of Order 2 with truth-value T. F.

And

$$\text{degree }(A_i) = \left\{\begin{array}{l}\text{Supremum }(p_1,p_2)\text{ as}\\ \text{well as (exclusive)}\\ \text{infirmum }(p_1,p_2)\end{array}\right\}$$

Where probability p_1 = 1 corresponding to truth-value T and the probability p_2 = 0 to the truth-value F.

Logico-Spatio-Temporal Matrix

	$d(A_1) = (0,1)$	$d(A_2) = (0,1)$	$d(A_3) = (0,1)$					$d(A_n) = (0,1)$
$X_1 = (r_1, t_1)$	$(r_1, t_1), 1$	$(r_1, t_1), 0$	$(r_1, t_1), 0$					$(r_1, t_1), 0$
$X_2 = (r_2, t_2)$	$(r_2, t_2), 0$	$(r_2, t_2), 1$	$(r_2, t_2), 0$					$(r_2, t_2), 0$
$X_3 = (r_3, t_3)$	$(r_3, t_3), 0$	$(r_3, t_3), 0$	$(r_3, t_3), 1$					$(r_3, t_3), 0$
$X_n = (r_n, t_n)$	$(r_n, t_n), 0$	$(r_n, t_n), 0$	$(r_n, t_n), 0$					$(r_n, t_n), 1$

This is a space-time matrix of Logical Manifold $L^2_{(0,1)}$ where order 2 (Macroscopic) of an Event (Illustrated above) *degree has 1*

The other space-time matrix of Logical Manifold $L^2_{(0,1)}$ where order 2 is an *empty event* is not therefore illustrate. *degree has 0*

So for the classical logic rests on the facit assumption that can apply informly to all events irrespective of their nature. The aim is to recognise the limitation of the traditional logic and points towards a "hetero-logical scheme" which can further clarify events in nature of the micro-world. I hope the diagram outlined below in future clarify events in the space $\{(R^3 \times T) \times L^n_m\}$ of the heterological approach.

Logic-Spatio-Temporal Space:

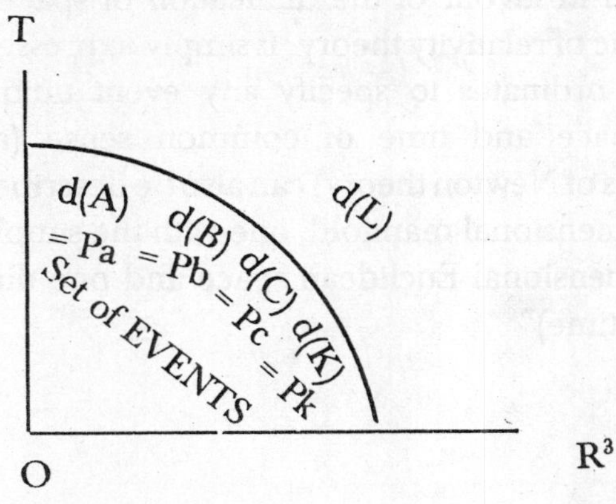

Appendix I

I begin the *seven dimensional Logico Spatio-Temporal Manifold** $(R^3 \times T) \times L^n_{(m_1,m_2)}$ by supporting my formula equation[(+)]

$(R^3 \times T) \underset{n}{\times} L^n_{(m_1,m_2)} = \{(x,y,z),t; [n, (m_1,m_2)]\}$ for (x,y,z) E R^3 t E T for $L_{(m_1,m_2)}$ is a Logical Manifold of Heterologic and $n \geq 1$(n..... natural numbers and 0), $0 < m_1 \leq 1$, $0 \leq m_2 < 1$ and `∈' denotes `belongs to' and `X' as Cartesian Product.

By quoting the following form M. Friedman**, "viewing space-time as a four-dimensional manifold does not prejudice the question in favour of the unification of space and time characteristic of relativity theory. It simply expresses the need for four co-ordinates to specify any event uniquely. The separate space and time of common sense (and some formulations of Newton theory) can also be described in terms of a four dimensional manifold, one with the simple product of three-dimensional Euclidean space and one dimensional Newtonian time)"

---

* We note that its *seven-dimensional* because apart from four-dimensional of $(R^3 \times T)$, we have the other dimensionals of one dimension corresponding the ORDER and two dimensions of DEGREE of logical Manifold say $L^n_{(m_1,m_2)}$ (See Sec.II)

** Foundations of space-time theories (Relativitic Physics, Philosophy of Science) Michael Friedman, (Princeton University Press, Princeton, New Jersey).

Appendix II

Heterological approach have observational truth-values which depend on concept of probability i.e. then the Supremum of observation truth-values ***materialise events*** and also we consider the infirmum of observational truth-values which ***may create*** an ***empty event***. Therefore we don't illustrate the space-time matrix in this case (empty event) (Since Logical Manifold $L^{2}_{(0,1)}$ with order 2 *but* has degree 0).

Bibliography

1. Indian Philosophy / J. Singh (Oriental Publishers)
2. Buddhist Theory of Causation and Einstein's Theory of Relativity / F. Bharucha, Delhi,1992. (Sri Satguru Publications).
3. Indian Philosophy / S.B. Dasgupta (Oriental Publishers)
4. Syadvāda Theory of Jainism in Terms of a Deviant Logic / F. Bharucha (Indian Philosophical Quarterly, Vol XI, No, 2 April 1984)
5. Deviant Logics for Quartum Mechanics / F. Bharucha (Indian Philosophical Quarterly, Vol XIV, No 1, Jan-March 1987- Nistada, New Delhi, 1988
6. In Quest of the Quantum / L. Ponomarrev. (Mir Publishers)
7. Redefining Universals / F. Bharucha (Indian Philosophy Quarterly-Vol IX, No 3, April (1982)
8. Thought Experiments in Philosophy and Physico / F. Bharucha (Visva-Bharati Journal of Philosophy XIV- No 2 1988; F. Bharucha XXV - No. 2 1988, (i) and (ii) World Philosophical Index
9. Foundation of Space-Time Theories / Michael Friedman (Princeton University Press)
10. World Enough and Space-Time / John Earman (M.I.T. Press)
11. Logic-Spatio-Temporal / F. Bharucha (Presented as a paper in Berlin 1992)